3/18   LG 0.8 0.5pt.

spot

MIGHTY MACHINES

BULLDOZERS

by Mari Schuh

AMICUS | AMICUS INK

blade

ripper

Look for these words and pictures as you read.

tracks

cab

Here comes a bulldozer!
What can it do?

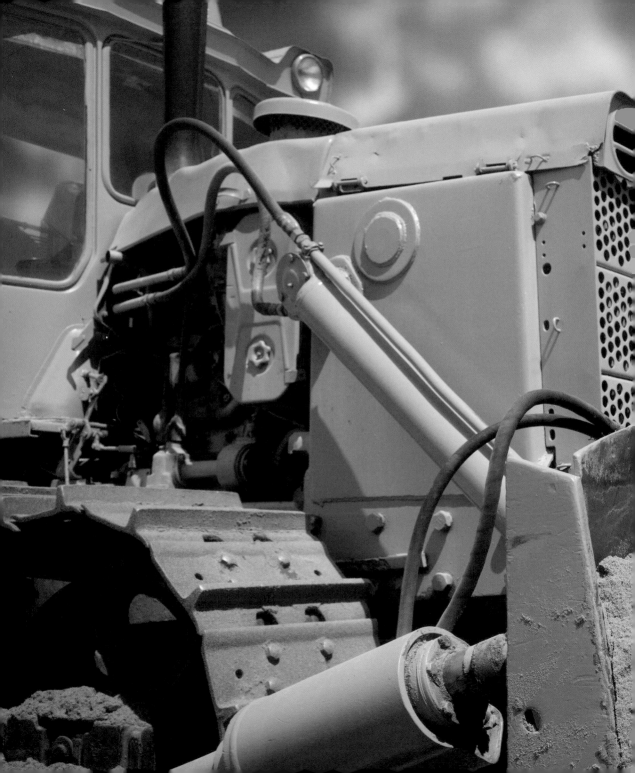

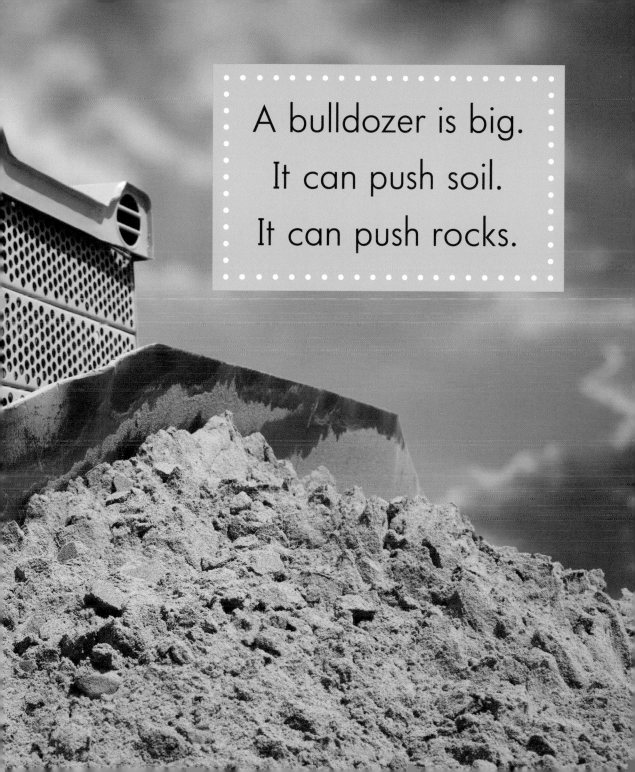

A bulldozer is big.
It can push soil.
It can push rocks.

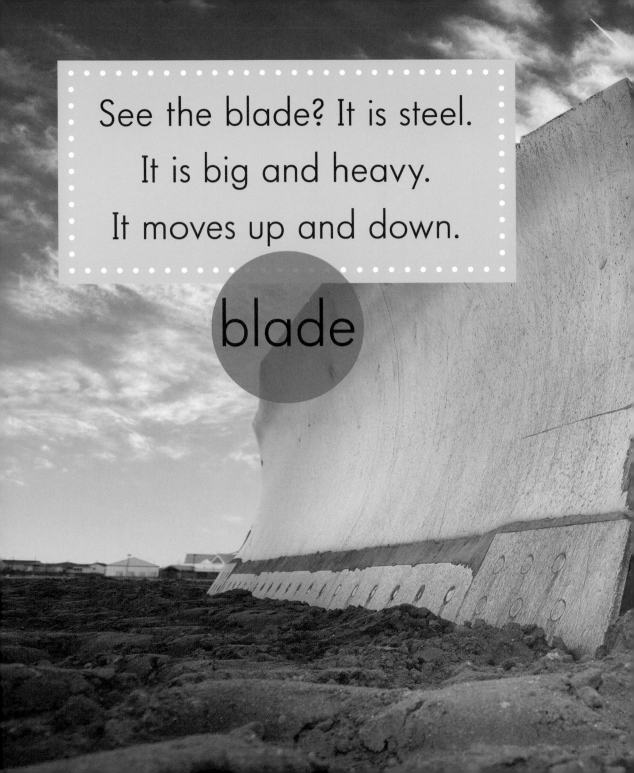

See the blade? It is steel.
It is big and heavy.
It moves up and down.

blade

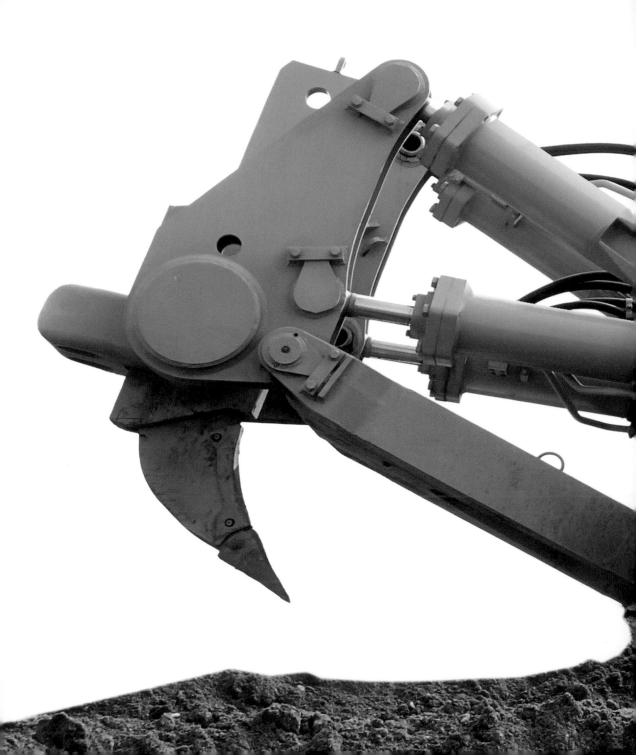

ripper

See the ripper?

It digs. It breaks up rocks.

It breaks up hard ground.

See the tracks?
They are wide.
They have ridges.

tracks

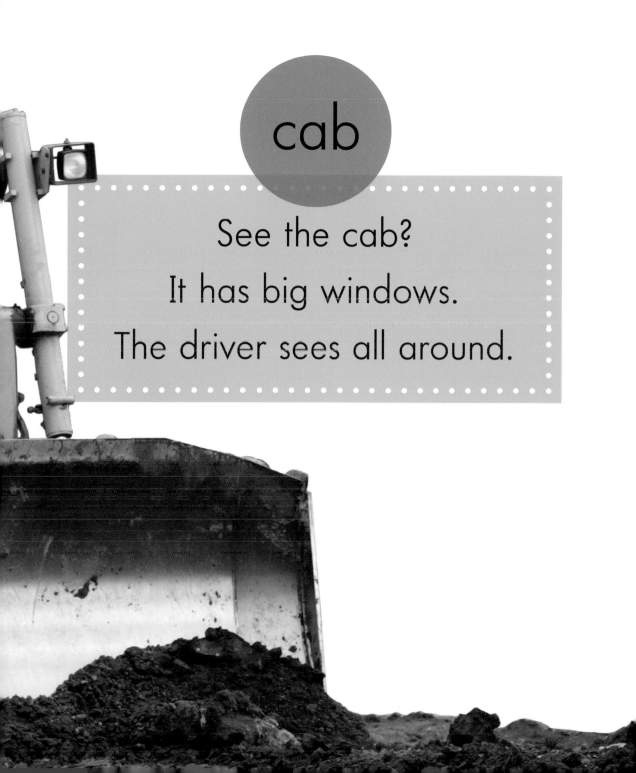

cab

See the cab?
It has big windows.
The driver sees all around.

A bulldozer is tough.

It is ready to work.

Let's go!

See the blade? It is steel.
It is big and heavy.
It moves up and down.
blade

blade

ripper
See the ripper?
It digs. It breaks up rocks.
It breaks up hard ground.

ripper

Did you find?

tracks

cab

See the tracks?
They are wide.
They have ridges.
tracks

cab
See the cab?
It has big windows.
The driver sees all around.

Spot is published by Amicus and Amicus Ink
P.O. Box 1329, Mankato, MN 56002
www.amicuspublishing.us

Library of Congress Cataloging-in-Publication Data
   Names: Schuh, Mari C., 1975- author.
Title: Bulldozers / by Mari Schuh.
Description: Mankato, Minnesota : Amicus, 2018. | Series:
   Spot. Mighty machines | Audience: Grades K-3.
Identifiers: LCCN 2016044415 (print) | LCCN 2016045612
   (ebook) | ISBN 9781681522104 (pbk.) | ISBN
   9781681510996 (library binding) | ISBN 9781681511894
   (e-book)
Subjects: LCSH: Bulldozers--Juvenile literature.
Classification: LCC TA725 .S38 2018 (print) | LCC TA725
   (ebook) | DDC 629.225--dc23
LC record available at https://lccn.loc.gov/2016044415

Printed in the United States of America

HC 10 9 8 7 6 5 4 3 2 1
PB 10 9 8 7 6 5 4 3 2 1

To Jadyn –MS

Wendy Dieker, editor
Deb Miner, series and book designer
Ciara Beitlich, production
Holly Young, production

Photos by 123rf 1, iStock cover, 3;
Sutterstock 4–5, 6–7, 8–9, 10–11,
12–13, 14–15